Other titles in the UWAP Poetry series (established 2016)

Infernal Topographies

Graeme Miles

Graeme Miles's poetry has been widely
published in Australian literary journals
and anthologies, and he has published
two previous collections of poems:
Recurrence (John Leonard Press, 2012)
and *Phosphorescence* (Fremantle Press,
2006). He has lived in Hobart since
2008 and teaches ancient languages
and literatures (especially Greek) at the
University of Tasmania.

Graeme Miles
Infernal
Topographies

Poetry

First published in 2020 by
UWA Publishing
Crawley, Western Australia 6009
www.uwap.uwa.edu.au

UWAP is an imprint of UWA Publishing,
a division of The University of Western Australia.

THE UNIVERSITY OF
WESTERN
AUSTRALIA

Copyright © Graeme Miles 2020
The moral right of the author has been asserted.
ISBN: 978-1-76080-120-5

A catalogue record for this
book is available from the
National Library of Australia

Designed by Becky Chilcott, Chil3
Typeset in Lyon Text by Lasertype
Printed by McPherson's Printing Group

 uwapublishing

MIX
Paper from
responsible sources
FSC® C001695

For Ali, Angus and Freya

Contents

I was the last one left

after the great extinction. The others
hung around as ghosts. Some
inexplicable necessity compelled me
to mark the exams of the deceased.
I graded my brother-in-law's Russian paper, knowing
neither he nor I knew Russian.
I wanted to write
something about all this,
a solipsist novella.
It seemed worthwhile,
the act of working,
writing something about a turn back
to the brief blank between thoughts
like turning a cheek toward the space just emptied.

Living on the Banshee

Ah those days when we lived
on our own zeppelin. It was quiet
when it moved and silent
floating at anchor.
We had percentile dice
and a detailed chart
to determine our moods.
We called it the Banshee
in an ironic moment
but when it burned into almost nothingness
it sounded just like they said:
thousands of stones,
acres of greenhouses.

Infernal Topographies

For a while I joined the club for people
who like to be close to great white sharks
but they'd get on your nerves with their ecstasies,
their mock-humble willingness to be devoured.
I moved to an island called Earthly Paradise
by estate agents, as cover for a name
famous for brutality. When it got busier
bookshops came where you could buy poems
and a newspaper called Conquest Times.
I wondered whether it could really be called that
but thought I might be living a memory
from some period of unselfconscious empire.
Was about to buy some living poets
until someone pointed to a new Berryman,
big and crisp and blue, since if
there's one thing certain from infernal topographies
it's the neighborly feelings between deaths and dreams.

Domestic Fauna

1: Wryneck

Name: Wryneck.
Description: The head is small but with
a long beak, somewhere between
an ibis and a toucan. The body is
a coiled spring, feet long
and avian.
    Movement: A jaunty, fairground
rhythm with a little hop like
someone preparing an awkward kick.
Diet/favourite offerings: Smooth
twigs twisted slightly at one
end. Marriages, especially first
ones. Childhoods, especially
first ones. *Sounds/cries*:
Difficult to describe but suggestive
of the word 'disconsolate.'

2: Visits from wild animals

There are crocs outside in great numbers.
Now and then we shoot some
to keep a decent distance. The sensation
is like cracking a prawn or crayfish
with your thumbs.
                        There's a lion
half-tamed who pauses as you open
the door for him. He sniffs something
below the reach of human nostrils
and comes back in, lies
down for a chin scratch.
Hot baths can't equal
the rough pleasure of his tongue.

3: Visits from extinct animals

And once a thylacine came. Something wolfish
in its long head, its fur thick
and rough. Something hyena-like
in its knowing eyes. It knew
it was extinct because of us
(one pale human looking
much like another) so we worried
when the kids wanted to stroke
its long jaw, mimic its drunken
walk. It was like meeting someone
whose suffering you'd heard about,
someone excluded come out
of the past. It could almost have been
a person disguised or a sleazy god
in an old myth, hidden in a skin.
It had the look of someone condemned
who knows he's innocent and has something on you.

4: Sphere

Another household creature, quieter
being, the sphere, whose movement
is a circumambient flowing,
who seems to feed on nothing, or quietly
on itself, diminishing imperceptibly.
Its mostly hollow centre,
an emptiness to revolve around.
It is something before gender, that will outlive
all animals, everything weak enough
to need to move. It is prior
and patient, runs kaleidoscopic
shapes across its skin. It's
billions of years before the wryneck.

In a Symbolist Mood

Distant, untouchable night is stooping
over fingers of street-lights
that push her away. And the children of night?
The children of night are in hiding
wherever the dark still is,
under their mother's gauzy veil
or in the street where an ambulance
just passed.
            I was drunk once
in a dream, years ago.
The bushfire sun was orange
and I said that I wouldn't
remember this.
            So disjunct things drop,
as you forget them, with an oily, lurid swirl
of dream, a little drum-roll on the lids of the eyes.

Your Hands – Jean Moréas

'Tes mains' from *Les Syrtes*

Your hands seem to emerge from a tapestry,
very ancient, where silver joins itself to gold,
where among the bizarre confusion of branches
the outline of an image hunches in relief,
telling me of beautiful abductions and royal orgies,
and tournaments of knights, that I find nostalgic.

Your hands with their nails, pink and cutting as a beak,
strong enough to have plucked, once, the harp and the rebec,
under the inlaid canopy of an arched portal,
opening its trellis of gold on the cool bloom of a valley
and, dripping with unction, dye their fine rings
of chrysoprase in the blood of huguenots.

Your hands with pallid fingers are like the hands of a saint,
dreamed by Giotto and piously painted
in a corner, quite obscure, of some basilica
full of gold copes, tapers, relics,
where I want to sleep, like a bishop
dead in a sculpted tomb, without fear and without remorse.

Heart of Glass

She's walking to a phonebox
in the 80s, when Blondie
had a heart of glass.
House keys in her hand
night cold
key cold. At the box
an elderly lady taps her shoulder,
demanding, with some argument she can't refuse,
one of the lesser organs, a spleen.
She talks her
into taking it from someone else,
someone without a key
to get out of the night,
no call to make.
                     And she goes
home, driven by the father
she'd phoned, unlocks the door
and begins to forget, listening to that song
on the radio, Heart of Glass.

An Archaism

Can't quite shake the image of some
dusty, wheezing figure, always coming
into being in the corner of the room.
An archaism among hallucinations, a hermit
who prefers 'eremite.' Look closer
and he seems to be made of interlocking
triangles. Every possible combination
of lengths and angles must be there
somewhere. You can ask him anything
and get some reply. But you never know
if the words coming back have passed
under the lamp of an actually thinking mind
or a machine for the generation of oracles,
one engineered from smoke, so fine the back
of one hand could disperse it, but ungrippable,
invincible because barely there. He coughs
like someone knocking in morse code.
And he tells you all his correspondences:
a perfume, a virtue, an image.
Names and orders of angels, a leader over each,
a series of doors, corridors, mazes
of playing cards and tarocchi, to paper over
what neither is nor isn't, where you can
pile up the negations as deep as you like.
There is a sound in each sphere,
bells, hammers, the polite,
always slightly inaccurate chiming of clocks. Names to call,
successions of names. An intangible machine,
calling for belief, never expecting it,

driving it away with its crazy certainties,
its grails and trances. What he has to say
is an art in its impracticality, its skills
that like tango can never be mastered.
It has always to border the diabolic.
Everyone must doubt if we
should really be here.

Gnostic Wing

In a disused wing of the hospital
is a gnostic chapel. The staff call it
the Evangelist's Nightmare.
Nothing much was happening there,
but the red Christ was almost un-
recognisable,

and some breeze was blowing a red
and black curtain. The priest mumbled
something about
being a passer-by, from the Gospel of Thomas.
Reminded me of a dream about escaping
an underworld

guarded by a juggler of colourful skittles,
polite but firm. Weighing up
mythic precedents
we'd ditched them all, scrambled
instead back up the dry throat
of the crematorium.

The Reed Man

Down among the reeds lives
     the reed man.
His smile creeks open like rushes
     part in the summer.
     For him the ideal offering
is honeycomb with a hint of affection.
Don't encourage or scorn.
     If you dig down there
among his plants and the rustling,
with long boots and an eye
     for tiger snakes, you'll find
the roots are edible, plump and red
     when the stalk withers.
By your boots the frogs moan
     quietly, knowing their place.
In the winter he's sodden to his wits.

A Bone of the Mother

To begin with liquid stone and heat,
fierce pressure. To be pushed up
through broken crust into bitter cooling,
edges forming between self
and not-self. Weather pulses
and performs above, you change only
by millenia. Flood comes and the sky
is filtered down to you through greens
and greys. And after the flood abates
you are thrown over human shoulders
to become like them. Mineral flecks
and veins become arteries, tendons,
nerves to report back every
least movement out there. You have to
breathe out and in with little pauses,
fill a belly to empty again.
If you discipline every cell and muscle
you can return for a moment to the fixity
you once had as brute, honest matter,
when you were just a mother's bone.

In What Sense Books Make Immortal

As you enter, the opposite door has just
slammed shut. Objects on the table,
in an attempt at neat lines, are just
abandoned. A mug's hot contents cool,
notebook is open and pages numbered
to 112, in the corner where the writer
numbers them four at a time
until the book's extinction. A book
by someone else is open nearby. (In it
another door has just been slammed.)
The light will fall like this
from now on and no one will see it.
The CD (such old technology)
won't be restarted.
　　　　　But whenever you arrive here
it won't be in the depths
of all the time after the departure
but just now – with the sound of wood
on wood and the high hinge.

Dreaming about Jiu Jitsu

It isn't what you don't know. That's just confusion.
Musashi, 'The Book of Void'

Dreaming about jiu jitsu now for twenty
odd years with such sameness, returning
to a class, the ageless sensei
still quiet, gentle, bearded, and that beard
still black, not grey or white as it must be
on the living man. The mats smell
of sharp straw.
          Begin kneeling
in a row of miniature samurai then roll
forward, backward, flat-falls. The locks
and throws. You are always the defender,
meditator on weight and motion, gravity
the concealed weapon. You practise knocking
blunt knife or wooden gun from a hand.
The body is information, all angles,
velocities. Even its tides are there
somewhere at the bottom end of awareness.
Arms are equations to be solved, and at
their ends are knuckles, digits.
The mind choosing the next block
or kick in the kata is zero.

Weight of Memory

My graduate student called from Melbourne.
She was at the conference. When
was I getting there? I had forgotten
the conference, to book a flight, to write
my paper (*Opisthobarês*. The weight of memory
in Neoplatonism.)

Searching for rooms, thumbing the glossy program
I found a little cemetery, a plaque
for a child. The bronze recorded
word for word my email replies
to a list of questions.

Somehow, hurrying, I'd forgotten.
I had given her place of birth and death.
'Favourite thing to bury with her?
Tiger.' Eye skips to dates.
2007. 8.

A Note on Water

There's a well under each house
where words are drawn up. Some are
just springs among bare rocks.
They taste of limestone and their sentences
move free of dirt and obstructions to their end.
They are like the lines of aged widows
on the other side of grief who have
their stone houses away from salt springs.
Or some are old, tall wells
of large brick in courtyards
where the water is still black
when you draw it up, and it tastes
of the predatory thoughts of millipedes.
Their logic is relentless and articulated.
They are how the world has always been.

Dog, Mountain and Moon

for Freya

Ask our daughter each morning what she dreamed.
Usually 'a dog, a mountain and the moon.'
She adds, 'I wasn't scared.'
But the children in the camps
with their sad pictures asking for help.
And if we too were driven out
by history with its money and bullets
I could no longer close our brittle gate
its brave little click
against it all. 'I dreamed
rain falling up and grandad's friends.'
But crowds have caught ship to ruined country
to be rebrutalised, sent back to their killers,
Palai, Tamil landscape of scratching out whatever's left,
skinny trees and garbage. 'Dog, wolf, moon and mountain,'
she says one day. 'I wasn't scared.'

Some Similes about Similes about Similes

They're like the portrait of a character
whose actions you know in detail but whose face
you've never seen. They're like the resolution
pointing its puny finger hopelessly
at stronger habits. Some are like results
from machines detecting accidentally
what can't exist on any understanding
of the world. Or like the sewing machine
that met the umbrella during surgery
when the operator's shocked, dissociative.
They're the photos of sketches of once living skin.

from Antipater of Sidon
(*Anthologia Graeca* 7.427)

Let's see whose grave this is:
no words anywhere on the stone,
just nine fallen dice. Four
in the throw called 'Alexander',
four more in 'flower of youth',
an unlucky one in 'Chios.'
Maybe they say 'even kings
in their chambers and handsome boys
have nothingness in the end.'
Or no, I think I'll hit the target
like a Cretan archer:
the dead man was from Chios, who chanced
on Alexander as a name,
and he died young. Someone spoke
so well of a dead boy
and a gambled life through numbers on bones.

Five Years

The sea is gone,
                taking its orcas, anemones.
It is a man in an aged raincoat
or an invalid
                whose window looks out on hot-houses.
What a day to have been dead
five years.
                This mist looks like taking everything.

An Effigy

He wheeled his totem with him everywhere.
Its wood was dull and red.
It buttoned his shirts so tight
no chest-hair showed, made demure
little sounds with its wheels, this thing
of wood and thatch. It had its modesty.
This vehicle, this effigy spread wide
its arms in just one pose. The tongue it spoke
was smooth beads tapping. And even when
he spoke like anyone, was non-committal
like anyone, it sat beside him
looking at you through its semi-precious stones.
It crooked his infant in one wooden arm.

Hands in George Minne

Like toasting with antique champagne flutes,
already cracked, to shake these hands.
They are shaped to touch their owner's face,
refined beyond use. And yet
they're perfect machines for grieving, for clutching
a still, bony infant.
The mother falls with him at a cursive tilt,
pointing always to six past the hour,
drags the unseen, living child beside her
as student in grief. Or there's the couple
negotiating the holding of a hand,
when no one can say which bone
belongs to which. Everyone knows
that grim play, 'The Lovers', is about to begin.

The Iconoclast

Last night they caught the iconoclast
outside our window. He'd stayed four months
gone out each night to chip slow
then fast at the sculptures in the garden,
fetish or fundamentalism. The sculptor
tours us through the damage in the morning,
shows us where he's repaired
the impossibly spherical breast of a Lakshmi,
one finger from the Ganesh they've been doing puja for
twice a day for weeks, and the snake-head
curled around the neck of an ascetic Shiva
outside our door. We'd barely noticed the chiseling
at two in the morning in this town of sculptors,
thinking someone had woken with an idea
as if getting up to write a few lines.
The sculptor says, 'I don't worry
about punishing him, the god will punish him.'
And after four months he's gone,
this bearded American, taking
the stolen pieces like a bag of teeth and charms.

Gravity Again (Bracchiation)

We climbed back up into the trees,
tall white gums that grew
in every direction at once.
Cockatoos screamed and nested
where they'd split. But when we'd climbed
a little you couldn't tell
which ways were up down across.
So I told the kids to feel
for the pull of gravity
on their skin and hair.

Croesus. Two days.

1

Day of the eclipse. Through foliage
sun's circles turn semi-,
reduce to lunate sigmas. A little
crow comes, adds up
how many days per human life.
For all the tracks you make
across them, ruts of the same
measures, never twice the same.
Mummified in money, you might stifle a shock or two,
avoid a broken limb. But gold
is heavy, promisory notes burn.
None of it avoids the dream that talks
quietly by the bedhead
(deaths of children.) When the crows
are quiet the cold season begins.

2

He asks questions of the priesthood,
barefoot, listening to oak leaves.
Sends people through the desert
where the oasis god with curved horns
says something not recorded. Before
serious questions Croesus tests
the signal.
        If there's a voice
it tells nothing but the end
that will be variously
remembered: immolation,
Hyperborea, reprieve.

All Those Shipwrecks

All those shipwrecks against shell blue,
appearing there, part lit machines.
is like the tilt of migraine sight.
for sailors' nutmeg dreams, sickness
They are mistakes where no one should
past all requests: your own worn oar,

the clouds have shapes of never quite
The way they tilt, the sinking ships
Some of them are the least excuse
hallucinations, rank with salt.
have been or are like deaths in space
a tumulus, a string of shells.

Party music says

'fuck you, I'm young,' playing for someone else
in this room that smells
of cigarettes and dry ice for the smoke machine.
And as the music is repeating, circling
a few of its words like someone coming to an end
you move slowly downstairs with a friend
on each arm, three kids dressed
in new man-bodies. Where A
is antibiotic and B is beer
A and B have cancelled you out.
Someone has been so careless on these stairs,
left sleep sitting here in the strobe-light
where anyone could trip over it.

from Callimachus (*Anthologia Graeca* 7.80)

Someone spoke, Heraclitus, about your death, brought
a tear to me, and I remembered how many times
the two of us on a couch put down the sun. But you
stranger from Halicarnassus, were ashes four ages back.
Still your nightingales are living and death,
who snatches everything, can't throw his hand on them.

While he spoke about the one beyond being

making even the most invisible layer of matter
out of its fullness. While he divided immaterial
causes finer and finer
                        the dogs
had worried their way through the wire
into the chook-house, glutted
themselves on skin and wings, shaken
and shaken until those kites
of bone and feather were still.

Remaining Procession Reversion

It starts with the point then line then plane
then VOLUME in all senses. The flood
rush of waters and the dams. Lights
flick on. Darkness will be turned away.
So it goes a while, an appearance
of stability in the constant roaring into being
until all reverts. The turn can be felt
(but only if you're still enough) like
the tide-change people are supposed to die on.
The sequence runs back.
                              The last
quick phases of collapse are like the point
of falling asleep or sudden dark
in central latitudes. The screens
and their bright images are falling,
all comfortable dissimulations
take on a final transparency. The edge
is not in the picture, the limit of sight.
The house was only held together
by our presence here, willingness to repair
a window, spread another skin of paint
against the weather. We are heavy
beyond bearing as we rush to singularity.
Look how our final stumbling revolutions
put their weight into slowing time.

The Washerwoman of Paradise –
Maurice Rollinat

To the sound of foreign music
of harps and clavecins,
while praise and songs
float through the crowds

she cleans the robes and swaddling clothes
in holy water in the troughs,
to the sound of foreign music
of harps and clavecins.

And the blessèd fingerbones
on their cushions can see her
pressing saints' surplices
and collarettes of angels
to the sound of foreign music.

Dunes

1

The dunes perform the same
mutations. In sands like these:
first swigs of furtive whisky
to dull a bit the self-consciousness
of adolescent kisses. You could come home
with insect bites or love bites
vivid on your neck. Always the same smells
of coastal scrub: acrid, yet food-like,
inhumanly elevating like an incense. Intimate
as bodies newly mature. A smell to fall
through your senses or linger there
before the mind fully apprehends,
or when you're dulled, fragmented. In that smell hangs
a night of naked swimming that must
have been moonlit (there were
glowing bodies in the shallows and the chance
you might be seen, there was shyness
still in everyone's eyes, stronger than prurience.)
The lighthouse on Rotto revolved, metronome
ticking under the loose and improvised.

2

Now and then I'm convinced
that I died at eighteen in a house
near the sea from too much bourbon.
Everything since has been one of those dreams
collapsing time and detail into the few seconds
before I'm gone. It began
with waking, dragging my nauseous body
to the thin, buffalo-grass lawn
and seeing the remorseless blue sky pulse
with the rhythm of blood-vessels
behind the eyes. Events followed
better than you'd predict, shaped by
wish-fulfilment, twisted a little
by normal anxieties. There's a tell-tale lightness
to it all, the body is only
fully there when it figures in the dream's plot,
is otherwise implicitly living its own
chemical life. The dream fades
a bit when I suspect what it is
and there's a furtive, lying feeling when I write
the date, knowing it's really '94.

3

Trees floodlit by streetlights against
the density of Tasmanian darkness
remind me of a night on acid
in '95. Then – more than epiphanic trees
against the sky and what's left
of me saying to strangers 'I wish
you could see what I'm seeing.'
We played random notes on someone's
ill-tuned piano, until the other party
with its back to us on the patio,
the car thieves and dealers, threatened
to beat us up if we kept on.
Lucas declared us wreckage, as description
and prophecy, but nothing could help
falling out right: sky, stars
and everything, and all the sharps and flats
and in the cool out on the patio
the bruises on those mangled boys.

Architectural Self-Portrait

It's not a house or castle
but some fortified egoism.
It knows its landscape –
windows point to the most oceanic views,
sunwards at the best hours for warming.
Beyond those last headlands
is the Southern Ocean, deepening wildness
to the unearthly pole, where the world
is most and least itself. The house
edges it like you might poise
on the rim of a black hole.
There's a basement
to discard into, rudiments of a workshop
to repair a dog-gnawed chair
or corrupted expanse of chicken wire.
House's senses are questionable, the alarm
is jammed, prone to explosions
at imagined movement and the screen
reads in its green letters
'fire lounge override.'

Variations

My brother died from a dirty needle in a dream
where the mundane necessity of calling everyone
made me forget that I'd never had a brother.
Neglecting that detail I thought how he looked
like my son, that he seemed to have died by mistake
like the friend who stepped out on a freeway
when his car ran out of fuel, or when she killed
herself, and he did, and he did. The same
taste to it all of rancid olive oil.
These variations on a species like
the apparitions of jellyfish – slow jet,
unlikelihood and venom.

Ornithomancy

The problem of a chorus of swans both or-
        nithomantic puzzle and textual cue.
They revolve around a sleeping, pregnant woman
        clockwise and make their two sounds
at once: their cry, their wing-
        whistle. They verge on migration.
The myth conflates those two species
        of white swan, all over
like the flash of white under a black swan's
        wing, hidden under its bushfire
body, in the dark between feather and water.

A Period Drama

The carriage is moving away down its lane
in a world that's suddenly made for TV.
The girl and her maid are in focus against
the stained-glass blur of trees,
improbably blue sky behind them.
A dream seeded by television.
Somewhere a musket is cocked.
It sits in common hands for a useless effort
like braces on the teeth of the drowning.

Expectant Weather

One of those humid days, a disappointment
of rain. With my head full of Norse
the crows or ravens seemed
just right as *hrafnar*. They had
gone quiet for the season. Grass trees,
paperbarks, snakes. A lake that
came and went seasonally. Blood-root
and the intimate smell of mud.
I walked there self-consciously, feeling
that the inner and outer moods meshed
with unusual exactness,
like the chiming close to a poem.
The scene was finished, in the way
that only curtailed things are finished:
one lake of a line of lakes,
their paths obscured by roads,
new houses in parallel,
black roofs denying weather.

A Sign

A piano plays *A Country Practice*
on the new colour TV.
I'm in bed. There's a loose thread
on the goodsniff blanket that I tie
around my finger and around. The finger purples.
I go out to panic.
                The scissors
are in the new house down the street,
the one we're moving to. So we run,
Gran and I, *Country Practice* forgotten,
in the night I almost never see.
Suburban streetlights draw our shadows long,
boy and woman and trailing blanket,
a prosthetic wing that won't shake loose,
a sign for 'solicitude' and 'panic.'

Vanishing Point

In a reeking public toilet
the green light of trees reflects
through glass cubes, images
of the liquidity of vision.
From a smoky mirror
your face coheres semi-enduring.
For a while you're the heart of those waters
or a little chip in stone
under water's slow erasure.
And always your eyes move
over surfaces as if they're
too buoyant to reach below.

They feel for the vanishing point,
imaginary zero where all lines meet.
Out the other side of it
the image reverses like negative numbers.
Two delimited worlds respond.

In an image on a discarded magazine a corpse
lies white against Victorian black.
His arm reaches just through
the surface of the page
to where you're standing,
while a little dog looks at him, doesn't catch
a sniff of any mirror-dog past vanishing
or anyone like you watching outside.

from *La Vie des Chambres* –
Georges Rodenbach

Obscuring shadow in the rooms, evening is
a messenger of terrors who won't be comforted;
in mourning, she clothes herself in the shadow and rags of the moon,
she unquiet; she of the cats held close
like the water of the treacherous canals where you drown yourself.
Obscuring shadow is the murderess of joy
who withers, scent of vanishing roses,
when she pours herself out from her black vials.
Obscuring shadow lodges herself in the twilight;
she descends to the soul that darkens itself;
on the cheerful mirror falls a funereal veil;
brightness, you'd say, is wounded and retreats
towards the window where a shroud of lace offers itself.
The shadow is black poison of a deathly sweetness.
And look how you shake and don't know why...it's the hour
when the freed flight of souls skims past us;
ah! how hard it is! and the fears, the imperious fears
shake up the phantoms in the curtains of the beds
and these sacks of rags with voluptuous scents
and the lamps below reopen their scars
who will begin again to bleed the shadows.
But the shadow defends itself against the frail lamps
thickening in the corners its somber force
– you hear the gnats burn up their wings –
and you suspect, as you see the death of tiny creatures,
that it's the obscuring shadow who takes revenge
because they loved more than her black vials
the sun who revives in the faithful lamps.

Bells speak the language of hammers

and each stroke strikes a nail in
somewhere unseen. They build a ladder
of tarnished crucifixes, up or down,
from one church tower to the next
or into the sweet damp under them,
or onto ledges and fire-escapes
where cats move like draughts pieces,
finding fortuitous lines of jumps.
In this room a creature bristles
under a man's skin,
and every conversation
in the distance is a row.

In Rodenbach

It's always an old city in the evening.
Outside are canals, sounds of churches,
cheerful music for someone else
and street lights accentuate darkness.
Meaning can catch on anything: movements
in the curtains, netted veils over beds,
the petal by petal suicide of a flower
in the next room. Only the portraits
speak – and it takes so long
to speculate their characters, specify
what they will say and how.
Symbols never ascend, point instead
to each other, to the unplayed piano,
to whoever sits in this room, senses tender
like sunburned skin to the smallest touch.

Sight-lines

at Kerry Lodge, King's Meadows

From here you can squint through the gap
where the curtains never close into the house
on the next hill. The shapes are wrong,
glimpses into a cave, reflections
on metal. Shadows loop
like free-styling arms. It should always
be evening here, the stone of the jagged
bridge deepening red. The house
points forward like an eye waiting
for a figure stooped and running
on the road, returns of the ones flogged
or shot, displaced by new sickness.
From here you can always be watching
through the waved glass that stretches
and cramps the hills, road, approaching
faces.
        And when the glass is shattered
to its last, smallest shards, everything
soft or edible disappeared
except one soft tongue of leather,
just convict stones left to the scrutiny
of whoever still cares for memory,
then the briared country,
tough but maltreated like a street-kid,
will hesitate between these markers
for a watchman's vision and the older lines
walked deeper into the ground,
hesitate between lines of touch
and lines of sight.

Gimme Now

So brash today this harbour,
its simple colours
impersonating Sydney with yachts
and long bridge and cars. Helicopters
whoosh, stalk news down river
to sea and islands. It all fizzes
in the eyes like a gin and tonic,
quick and expensive with a promise
of more. It's the present saying
kiss me, how could I ever be different?

Chameleon

The people who lived here before
had a pet chameleon. Ugly thing,
our landlady says. They painted
the kitchen bright red, lounge
yellow, bathroom grass-green.
We're not sure if that was
for the chameleon or its owners.
When they moved out they left it
running loose, six floors up.
No more walks on a leash
on the terrace, no more
frozen grasshoppers in the freezer.

Vehicle

A mortal and a god step into
a vehicle. The god of course disguised
as the mortal's mortal friend. Could be
Athena or Krishna
(blue skin of the blue hour that seeps
into houses in Hobart in evenings
and now into this car, or grey eyes
of the owls you hear

but never see.) Whichever god's hiding
in that skin can strip shadow
from an eye. When a god goes
into a human skin
it needs a little ambrosia
to cover the weird smell, the ripe
reek that hints at its ending.
But there's a deeper pleasure

in the mortal machine, like an inhalation
to the lung-tops, held there a moment
so you feel any tiny scars.
That human skin
engulfs like the sea might
in some lyric poem, a bright
Pindaric thing. The god sitting
beside you

must be feeling something like that,
insists on driving as gods do.
Axles creak and your own limbs
are so heavy.
Yet you're electric fragments that tumble
down and up the spine, occluding
each other, entangling too.
You seem

to have the vapours, but your driver
rolls down a window and you feel
clear a moment, able to see
the freak chance
that any of these people on the street
were born, to see some self-indulgent diner
consuming all of them, and every building
and all the ivory

that anyone could poach, and all the fish
and octopuses with their weirdly human eyes.
That consuming thing pretends to be
a connoisseur.
You're shaken, the god can see that,
so pulls over. By way of consolation
you're allowed to look down into
the driver's mouth.

Instead of the homely apparatus
of digestion, you see how it's alright
that worlds devour themselves, that some
old fault
in ape-kind can't help but poise
its everything on a final drop, pretending
it'll save itself at the last chance.
You know

it's okay that the millions of years
between extinctions run through,
and you see inside that mouth
yourself looking in,
your shoulders relaxed, eyes fixed
on the shifts from cells and thermal vents
to eyes and mouths, and thoughts about thoughts
about thoughts.

The Frames

for Ali

As it blooms out of matter
you can catch consciousness
just as you wake
coming from brute silence
the long night to be slept through.
My mind along with yours beside me
is moved into place and illuminated.
It happens at just the same moment
for just the same few years.
A squat shrub near the sea
blooms film and daylight picks out those squares,
the world is mechanism and projectionist.
As you wake it's clearly okay
that each frame perishes,
flames or fades.

The Twins

A rich man wanted to be
poised at the moment of sunset.
In a custom orbital craft
above the airlines, refueled
by a fleet from every country
he suspended the moment. The staff
perform their functions with gin and canapes
(always the hour for Gs and Ts) and disappear,
ageing imperceptibly. Their master,
their Flying Dutchman, rides
on that gasp of a moment. His twin,
in a craft identical in every respect
sits in the other hemisphere,
revolving at the moment of sunrise
on an opposite gasp of expectation.
They never meet, like Night and Day in the Veda,
living separately in one house.

A few roos loose in the top paddock

so keep dogs leashed. You need
to manoeuvre them towards the gates
that they always seem to run past,
use their flightiness to move them
while they hover above the ground,
extending legs just to beat out a rhythm.
Like Wittgenstein's fly in a bottle
to be tricked out with philosophy
the roos can't be approached directly.
Releasing them is a work of obliquity,
of setting the available people
in a pattern of deflections, like stanzas,
like pinball. Eventually, maybe just by luck
to let them out.

Polemo Dies

As they shut Polemo live in his coffin,
on his own orders, he had to give
just one more line: 'Hurry,
the sun mustn't see me silent.'
A sort of heroism, his biographer thought,
to be in pain and at the end,
still think the half-joking pose
worth striking. And he'd thought others' deaths
worth a cute line (the gladiator who looked
fearful as a sophist waiting to declaim),
as if there were only words to fear
or be joyful over, and even Polemo would soon
be just a theme. Or else he was too busy being
Polemo to feel the animal sameness of his death.

From a Colony

Here stones, there sea. Some
hills, a river. Enough to make a world.
In the river flecks of gold so the people
come and from the hills watch
each other moving. On this hill
they see a horse, say *esva*,
on that hill say *hippos*. The head man
of *hippos* meets head man of *esva*.
Hand shoves into soft chiton. Hand shoves
into leather. *Esva*-chief falls under kicks
from lanky kids at *hippos'* side.
Everyone watches. And the *esva*-folk decide
not to go to the *hippos*-hill with long knives
but join them, use them against the others.
And in years they bury the *hippos*-chief
under their hill, remember him
with black goats and warm blood.
Under *esva*-hill they hide their man-god
swallowed by the earth, the horseman
murdered in his sleep. They watch
from the hills, and in the pits and on low altars
warm blood and black fleece, sand.
Hands are shaken tight as strangling.

After Damascius

In the old days they hadn't even heard of it,
reading the future in clouds.
It was Anthousa, whose husband
was fighting in Sicily. Her father told her
in a dream, to pray to the rising and
the setting sun. A cloud came
from a clear sky and formed a man,
a Goth, and from it a lion
to eat the man. And the emperor
Leo murdered his enemy
and his sons and Anthousa's husband
came home. She went on reading clouds
up to now, to this very day.

Gaming

for Jeff

Those toy men kill each other in a landscape
you have drawn from movies about Vietnam.
(In friends' houses the fathers and uncles try not
to pass on reflexes like grenades.) We're grown kids
so our game is complicated by probabilities, dice,
range of weapons and effects of terrain.
This is not playing soldiers, it's a War Game.
You ambush me and easily win. I lose
as North Vietnam.
                 We play another game
of Dungeons and Dragons, and Death chases you
with his cartoon scythe through a maze I've made.
Almost by accident the game has real fear,
as though he will come into whatever shape
will fit. These lesser rituals rehearse us
for the growing fall, our biggest, final game.

Scottish Gothic

for Ali

Whether because of limitations of this dark, local stone,
its heaviness, its hint of blood,
or some gnosticism of the local imagination,
the gothic here never soars, just hovers a little shy
of earth, not Platonic like the dialogue
of stone and form in Flanders or France,
but a gargoyle's view of it,
foreshortened through a heavy, stone-cut eye.

The Inevitable Elegy

i.m. Lucas North

Es ist Nichts
Es ist Nichts
Es ist Nichts
Es ist

– Einstürzende Neubauten, 'Dead Friends'

If you called me up again
late at night with your raspy voice
to ask my address so you could send
your hilarious, terrifying cartoons
('I have a cause and a pipe-bomb')
it would take me a moment
to remember it's impossible.
You're still out there
and this is why when I try to feel
whether someone at the other end
of a long severance is alive or dead
I just can't tell, since even the ones
definitely gone are still live on the line,
my friend of the long phonecall.

I remember your books of unusable characters,
plots like machines to solve a problem
no one ever thought of. Your walls
of sticky notes and diagrams
like a cop's incident room.
The names were ludicrous on purpose:
Chirp McBurger, Drive Thru Man.
It was always night in a suburb
or industrial area, the patchily
fluoro-lit edges of the time,
its 'blind devotion to the wheel.'

Twee

I was travelling somewhere for a conference
and it was green and historic.
There was a twee-ness
a Tolkien-look to the landscape
and the carefully preserved menace
of its castles. Everything seemed
to have been framed by someone else
like a quotation. I went into a historic site
and was suddenly lost,
couldn't remember how one curated room
related to another. The guides
took me out like a damaged relic,
mind dissolving in the stained glass colours,
blessing the indulgent waters of Twee,
as someone wrote a brilliant footnote on that word.

Hunting the Alien

There's someone I'm always looking for
through the endless poems, line
after line. Each one is an excuse
and opportunity. Each might just be the one
that gives more than resemblance and deflection.
Each is in the end like the time as a kid
I was convinced that aliens must be nearby
and spent some long, vague time in the park
looking quickly around trees and bushes, sure
I'd surprise one this time, but only seeing
white flashes in the corner of my eye.
It was something short enough
that it didn't threaten, big enough
it might be one of them.

Constructing Mornings

Waking each morning calls you to remember
where in the plot this is, like slowly reading
one of the old, inherited epics
whose story you seem always
to have known, but you wonder
how tough-minded the poet has been
in this episode, whether necessities of plot
allowed the characters to be spared a little.
Details of touch and hearing slowly cohere
like tenses of verbs, cases of nouns
in the present sentence. There's our dog
shaggily alive in his mid-years and sounds
of half-grown children making something
in another room. There is the temperature
steadily rising.
                    These long lines ought
to be read unhurried, allowing caesurae
to pause then tip into asymmetry,
not hurrying to little triumphs, grotesques
half-hidden in the poem's sheer length.
The fact of morning hangs there as an absolute –
around it move details of a house and heat.

Dry Lightning

Watching dry lightning move
from behind the wooded hill just there
to the Eastern shore to the Peninsula,
I teach the kids to count between flash
and bang, tell them it's beautiful, and it is
the shattering blitz of it, rolling tympanon.
We don't know its fires will burn
for weeks, smudge out the sky
in the Huon and Highlands, move further
and nearer to my parents' house with turnings back
of wind. Each rising degree will bring
more of this.
        Its clouds are like
the ones supposed to come at endings
when distinctions fade, colours are
all the same and whatever sleeps
under it all, ruminating universes,
pulls clouds and lightning back
to itself, like a pillow drawn close.

Salt and Ash

It's raining now in the house that burned down this morning,
the one built in the year of the Symbolist Manifesto.
We saw the thick grey smoke of old wood
and heard what metal was left of the roof squeak
as it tightened under the water of firehoses.
The house that was for sale,
whose simulacra are still intact
in the estate agent's window
is all outside now as graves are.
The house where coaches stopped
on their way to the Huon, let down
a limp, thick arm of smoke,
pointed to the gap where the Southern Ocean starts.
Bury its ashes between high and low tide.
Salt seal it against unhappy returns.

Dream Genres

1: More Rooms to the House

1

He's forgotten until today a door
in the weatherboard bungalow.
Through it there's another wing to the house,
a ballroom from the 1820s
where high stairs and tall ceiling
are cold above. He could sit
and write, now the kids wouldn't hurt
themselves in here, he could wear
thermals or light a fire. Behind
the ballroom stairs go down
to a derelict passage, out of sight
of the portraits in their steadfastness.
He says to anyone he meets outside
that finding it was like a common dream,
More Lost Rooms to the House,
one his friends had had, he'd
dreamed himself. Everything flickers,
becomes a bit unreal as he says it.
In that room before lightbulbs
night is unmitigated and snaps
each little thought with its brutal thumb.

2

To that century belong all passages
hidden under pubs and courthouses
on this island where the bricks
record prisoners' hands. It's no library
that he's found or kitchen, not even
the passage to escape a tribe reclaiming
land, to run hidden to the river.
An empty ballroom, bubble of peak years
of theft and slaughter. It's an opium dream
of Berlioz in an armour of dust.
'See me here,' says the note he slips
out under the heavy door, 'don't
see me here hiding in the past.'

2: Dead Friends

1

If there were a Feast of the Suicides
it'd be the busiest day for visiting.
My friend is back, still alcoholic
and ambushing people as a fleshy ghost.
I don't forget even for a moment
that he's dead. The debris
of his last years has settled,
and we can see again the old core
of friendship, shared mischief. He's still
somehow employed, despite his death
and resignation, so we pose together
for a university calendar for the coming year:
he is a monstrous robot, I'm
mock victim in his crushing claw.

2

There's always someone else to meet
at the conference where it doesn't matter
if you're alive or dead. My colleague
asks me to look after Marshall
while he himself works on disappearing into
his singularity. From some things
even the most unresolved of spirits
won't return. But Marshall seems
to need no care. His specialties
are bullets and blow darts. He's present
to inflict pain. Better leave him,
stay in the corner for those withering away,
remind them, just once more, their names.

3

They remade Lucas as a computer image.
It was on the news. The newsreader said
'the cricketer's brother' had been simulated
with original mannerisms. It cut to Marcus
(after recounting batting statistics
in this last few minutes after sport and weather)
standing beside the reconstruction.
I guess they asked him to smile
against a green screen, doing his best
to look fraternal. The image itself
was disappointing – face was right
(the easy bit) but gestures, expressions
exaggerated beyond anything
I remembered. No one had managed
to replicate his splintering voice.

3: *Trying to Get Back*

1

An old hotel in the country, evidently
in Europe, probably France. The colours
of walls and furniture are soft but glow
like the lightshow they project
at night on the Ara Pacis, showing
what it might have been. The beds are old
and too soft and I decay into them.
It's night and food
is brought by a man who lost a hand
in some old accident. The manager
is fiercely free from character, is the son
of a mother famous for toadstools and fingernails
ground down to charms.
                              It's been night for years
though only children are naïve enough
to say. Adults remark only the things
that go on despite the suffocation
of the light.
               Outside it was never France,
it was Australia, the southeast where
if you squint it could be almost Europe.
That could be a nothofagus, a pool
just frozen.
            The basement has a model
of the solar system, each planet is a sphere
revolving. The interstellar spaces are

reduced to the homely fixed stars, currently
in need of repair, jammed sometime
in the debauched and terrible reign
of the hotel's last owners. The model
has been useful in the years of the Eclipse,
(as they call it if they accidentally tell
some story that depends on knowing that
there once were hours of daylight.)
Outside it's near Perth, somewhere
like Serpentine, a night in summer
with a predicted storm that might arrive this time.
In a drawer in one room live a populace
of silverfish on what's left of a wedding dress.
They're so many for the little food left for them.
Outside is the nearly tropical air
of Sydney and the rhythm of cicadas
sounds wrong if you're from any other place.
You try to look to your lover's face but there's always
something else: your eye caught
by that bedside lamp reflected in the mirror,
or there's a sound, very clear, at the upper end
of your remaining hearing, or you're afraid
of how your look will be returned, or you
recall how many hours were spent on that
almost eaten wedding dress.
                              Outside
it has always been Tasmanian winter,
Jupiter and Saturn revolve just like
their polished simulacra in the basement.

It's a dark where past murders seem
so new, and night allows the island's
innocent animals to feed on skittled flesh.
They're sepia things in an archive, they're
growing native to the Long Eclipse.

2

Getting back is always the intention.
They've built new malls and cafes
where there used to be the union office
and pub. Same block of flats is there,
its dowdy 70s brick. But the balconies
look safer, where there was thin metal
against the drop (and you knew
how the pips of watermelons fell
from a child's mouth up there.)
The view is tidier, even Freo Harbour
and the cargo ships.
                              But there are barriers
between you and that flat, no way
to the lift with its sulpherous light
where you might well be stuck on your way
to the seventh floor, where a grandfather might
name you of all the children 'gentleman.'

3

He is translating Auguste Andaleuse,
drop-out from the nineteenth century,
would-be troubador on the back roads
of France and Italy. Short poems pooled
in the odd pages of his memoir. And the best of them
were written when he walked to the Community,
semi-monastery of not quite monks
and nuns, somewhere near Verona. His wife
had died long before and he walked
with his little daughter till their shoes
fell apart and feet ached. They grew
sicker as they went, convinced it was due to
'the cool, fresh water near Verona.'
They walked imagining handmade books
and stained glass, rooms safe and clean,
probity like an imaginary knight's code.
(Here he sounds like early Moréas.)
When they arrived she died and he
lived, made stained glass since there was
none, bound books and wrote the epitaph
to inscribe on her little stone just inside the walls.
Now and then,
the note says, a visitor on the long trail
of Andaleuse visits to see the stone,
or historians come for what's left of the Community.
He left behind her rucksack with her toys
and a few books, and his poem on a death and a well,
'the cool, fresh water near Verona.'

4: In the Vicinity of the Temple

1

A stone church like a mountain
in the country, near the sea.
It was built from tiny bricks, each
just a palm-full of grey flint.
You could move them one by one
with enough patience and forever on your hands.
It's dark inside to eyes closed by summer,
open just enough to let in the sallow.
Down the cliff over a shallow reef,
cerebral twists of coral and sea-grass –
the man-length of my father swimming.

2

The buses run almost to the peak
of Everest. It's busy up there with tourists
like me. The queue for the last flight
of stairs is long, the peak
crowded, the approach worn smooth.
Somewhere nearby, on a lower,
more secret peak, I went with a friend
whose year ahead was a shifting prognosis.
We thought we could feel our personal dead.
Things were fading down on our world's
mixing board, and we didn't know if
we were too. Or else we'd be left
in the dark, listening to silence after.

3

They gave me the hammer to show I was a killer.
I couldn't remember but went to hide it
somewhere away from cameras, not in a bin
that would go to the tip that junior cops
would go to search. Not in water
they'd dredge. Nowhere was secret enough
for my hammer and its bloody rag.
And so to trial and the punishment reserved:
I was spared the kid quick with a razor
who'd take just a little of you
with a snick almost like a joke.
It was human sacrifice for me, as though I were
a king of the woods to shake
a golden bough, to go down
through clouds of text, be translated
to an underworld. I knew it was right that I nod
when they sprinkled my forehead, pretend
there was no knife under the barley grains
in the basket. Pretend above all
to know my guilty conscience and my nerve.

4

I left a meeting in a back room
where the others were just silhouettes.
I had only loved them for a moment
when we all raised our shadows' fists
in solidarity.
                    So I wasn't sorry to go
back to Ghent in winter and walk
without much thought into Sint Baafs.
It was warm and blind black in there
and the heating shuddered a moment
when I hit the wrong switch. I crossed
myself and genuflected trying the gestures
on for size, bracketing all other issues.
When the lights came on the pews
were crowded with people silent and watching.

5: The End of It All

1

I dive where I used to walk, revisit
submerged places by snorkel. The beach
where half the suburb used to be
in Hobart summer, and where our dog walked,
is sandy bottom now for whiting.
High Street, where I was a toddler,
drowned under quick glugs of sea –
you can still spot asphalt, square edges
of a foundation. I'd like to think I dived
to the steps where I used to throw things down.
I went back to Oostende, swam
to the monument for Ensor, the crooked metal
cube and masks, more disorienting now
at the limit of breath in cold water. Fish
whose gray names I don't know swim through it.
The Descent of Ganga and the Shore Temple
at Mahabalipuram are smooth and magnified
through glass and water. The ascetic floats
the worlds and gods around him. Near home again
my friends' stone house, its witchy brooms
and dried body of a stingray from a beach,
its shelves of poems and philosophy, rooms loose
and long, are all returned to Great Oyster Bay.

Like in dementia the edges disappear bit
by bit, sometimes in rushes as ice
has melted somewhere distant,
and things drown from
complicated failures out of sight.

2

Sleeping through the longest lunar eclipse
in a century I dreamed it instead.
I saw the moon redden and darken
but when it was magnified
just above the horizon it became
a screen with features of the earth
projected on it. They were stretched
like in the back of a spoon.
I saw the red and rough of central Australia
as some play of angles showed
the continent nearest. The moon
distilled the earth into its powder and shadows.
I remembered a tree during a solar eclipse
dissolving discs of sun as the shadow moved,
making medallions to commemorate
the sun the sun the sun.

Acknowledgements

Some of the poems in this collection have appeared in the following publications: 'In a Symbolist Mood' (*Australian Book Review*); 'Domestic Fauna' (*Cordite*); 'Heart of Glass', 'An Archaism', 'The Iconoclast' (*Southerly*); 'Dog, Mountain and Moon' (*Writing to the Wire*, eds. Dan Disney and Kit Kelen); 'Some Similes About Similes About Similes', 'Ash and Salt' (*Westerly*); 'All those shipwrecks' and 'From a colony' (*Otoliths*), 'Infernal Topographies' (*Island*); 'In Rodenbach' and 'While he spoke about the one beyond being' (*Stylus*), 'I was the last one left' (*Meanjin*). The sequence 'Dream Genres' was written on commission from the *Red Room Company* and 'Sight-lines' for the *Lines of Sight: Kerry Lodge Exhibition – Launceston*. This collection was written on Noongar and Palawa land. I acknowledge the traditional owners and pay my respects to their ancestors, elders and families, their languages and the wisdom in them, past, present and in perpetuity.